Optimism

Optimism

TEXT BY CHRISTIAN LARSON

COMPILED BY WELLERAN POLTARNEES

LAUGHNG ELEPHANT · MCMVII

LAUGHING ELEPHANT

www.LAUGHINGELEPHANT.com

Promise Yourself...

To be so strong
that nothing can disturb
your peace of mind.

To talk health,
happiness and prosperity
to every person you meet.

To make all your friends
feel that there is something in them.

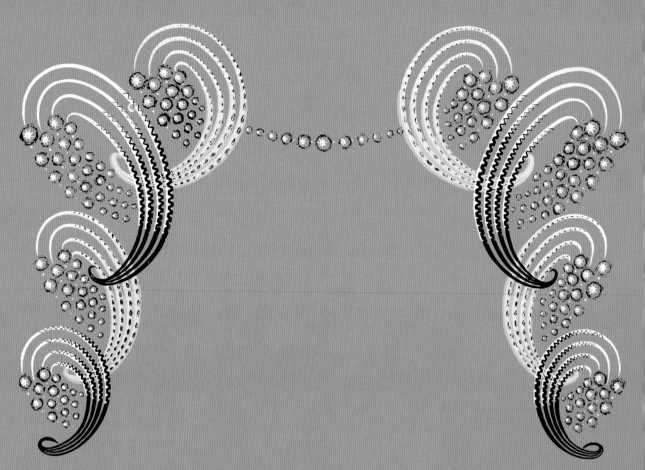

To look at the sunny side of everything

And make your
optimism come true.

10

To think only of the best,
to work only for the best,
and to expect only the best.

To be just as enthusiastic about
the success of others
as you are about your own.

To forget the mistakes of the past
and press on to the
greater achievements of the future.

To wear a cheerful
countenance at all times.

18

And give every living creature
you meet a smile.

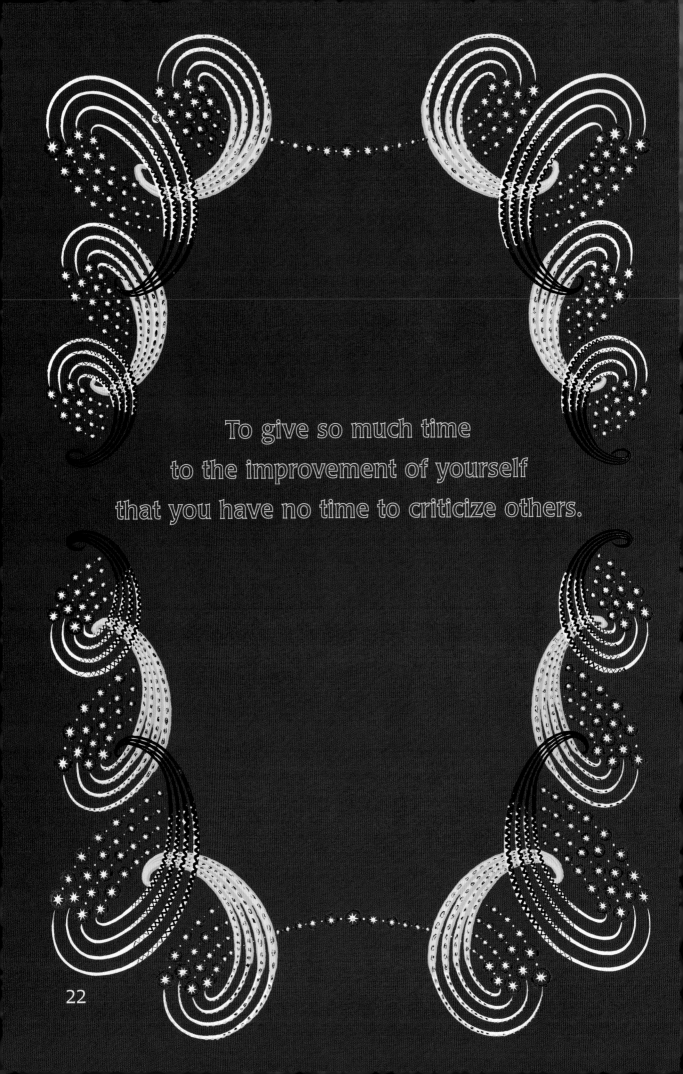

To give so much time
to the improvement of yourself
that you have no time to criticize others.

23

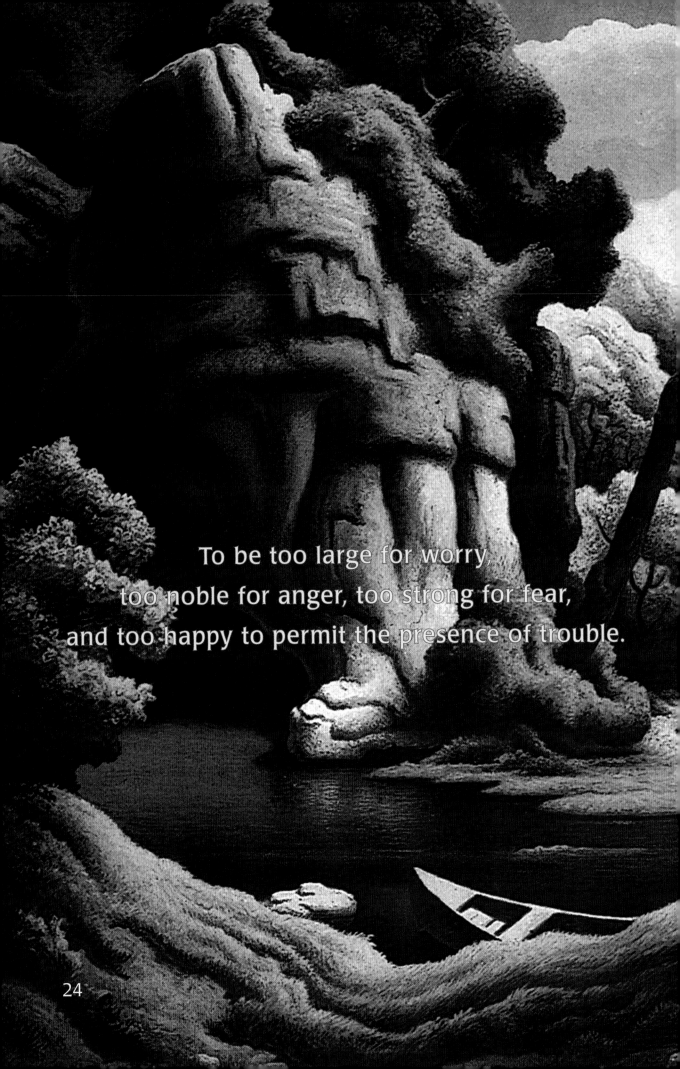

To be too large for worry,
too noble for anger, too strong for fear,
and too happy to permit the presence of trouble.

24

Promise yourself.

26

PICTURE CREDITS